POINTS AT ISSUE

A Bookseller Looks at Bibliography

A Lecture delivered at the Library of Congress on April 24, 1984

by Anthony Rota

Library of Congress
Washington
1984

The Center for the Book
Viewpoint Series
No. 12

This booklet is printed on acid-free paper.
Designed by Hausmann/Krohn, Inc.
Typeset in ITC Berkeley Oldstyle Book by
Composition Systems Inc.
Printed in an edition of 2,000 by Printing Incorporated

Library of Congress Cataloging in Publication Data

Rota, Anthony.
Points at issue.

(The Center for the Book viewpoint series; no. 12)
"One in the series of Engelhard Lectures on the Book"—Pref.
Bibliography: p.
Supt. of Docs. no.: LC 1.38:12
1. Bibliography—Methodology—Addresses, essays, lectures. 2. Literature, Modern—Bibliography—Addresses, essays, lectures. 3. Booksellers and bookselling—Addresses, essays, lectures. 4. Rare books—Bibliography—Methodology—Addresses, essays, lectures. I. Title.
II. Title: Engelhard lecture series on the book.
III. Series: Center for the Book viewpoint series; 12.
Z1001.R77 1984 010'.4 84-600230
ISBN 0-8444-0471-3 (alk. paper)

PREFACE

On April 24, 1984, Anthony Rota delivered a lecture at the Library of Congress titled "Points at Issue: A Bookseller Looks at Bibliography." The presentation was sponsored by the Center for the Book in the Library of Congress, which was created by Act of Congress in 1977 to focus national attention on the importance of books, reading, and the written word. The history of books, reading promotion, and the role of books in contemporary society are its three major interests. An informal, voluntary organization funded primarily by private contributions, the Center for the Book brings together members of the book, educational, and business communities for projects and symposia. Drawing on the collections and specialists of the Library of Congress, it also sponsors publications, exhibitions, and events that enhance books and reading in our society.

Mr. Rota's talk is one in the series of Engelhard Lectures on the Book, supported by Mrs. Charles W. Engelhard. The series of public talks considers books in their many roles—as they exemplify the graphic and typographic arts, as they are described by bibliographers, used by scholars, and sought by collectors, and as they stir the imagination, transmit ideas, and shape society. The tenth in the series, Mr. Rota's talk is the first one to deal directly with bookselling.

Anthony Rota is director of the distinguished rare book firm Bertram Rota Limited in London. His observations are based on his thirty-two years' experience with the company, which was established by his father, the late Bertram Rota, in 1923. The firm specializes in first editions and original manuscripts and letters of English and American authors. Over the years biographers and bibliographers of nineteenth- and twentieth-century authors have regularly acknowledged the assistance Mr. Rota has given them in his work. Drawing on his own experiences, he considers the contributions that both booksellers and bibliographers make to literary scholarship. It is a pleasure to present his candid and engaging observations to a wider audience and to acknowledge the support of Mrs. Charles W. Engelhard in making this series possible.

John Y. Cole
Executive Director
The Center for the Book

POINTS AT ISSUE:
A Bookseller Looks at Bibliography

Bibliography is like the Irish question: it is long on problems and short on solutions. I want here to look with you at some of the problems.

If the role of the bookseller is to put the right book in the right place, it follows that he supplies much of the raw material for bibliography and is, both on his own account and on behalf of his customers, a market for the finished product of bibliographical research. It is from my twin viewpoint of supplier and consumer that I want to survey the bibliographical scene.

When I speak of *bibliography*, I shall for the most part be referring to descriptive bibliographies devoted to individual authors of creative writing during the last hundred years, which is to say the period of machine-made books, but I hope my remarks will not be without relevance in other fields of bibliography.

I want to talk first about what the bookseller has to offer the bibliographer—apart from the books on the bookshop shelf—and then about what I for one ask from the bibliographer in exchange.

What the Bookseller Can Offer the Bibliographer

It is one of the unfair things about this life that what the bookseller can offer the bibliographer is tenuous, sketchy, and blurred at the edges, whereas what he wants from him is something clear-cut and precise. On the evidence so far before me, I am by no means convinced that booksellers make good bibliographers. There are honorable exceptions to this rule, I have no doubt, but when Dan Laurence discussed his own work on Bernard Shaw on this platform in November 1983 he rightly castigated much of the second-rate work, some of the bad bibliographies by booksellers, as "repositories of semidigested information, questionable assumptions, and hasty conclusions."[1] On the other hand, one has only to turn to the acknowledgments section in almost any twentieth-century bibliography to see the generous terms in which the compilers express their gratitude for the help that booksellers have given them. For example, in the second edition of his *Bibliography of D. H. Lawrence*, Warren Roberts went so far as to say, "Bookdealers usually know more about the intricacies of Lawrence books than the scholars who work with them. . . ."

The truth of the matter is that the bookdealer certainly has the *opportunity* to know more. In the course of a working lifetime he tends to handle many, many copies of the relatively common books and more copies than most people of the rare ones. His difficulty is that in the nature of things, he does not have them all in front of him at one time and thus is not able to make detailed technical comparisons. When our bibliographer tours the copyright deposit libraries and the great collections, he can check each copy he sees against a meticulous description of those he has seen before. In this imperfect world the dealer probably relies on a combination of memory and hunch. Thus he may be able to say, "I am sure the last copy I had was in a paler shade of cloth" or "Something about the lettering on that spine looks different to me." If the bibliographer is lucky, his dealer friend will—eventually—turn up an old catalog entry to prove his point.

If a bibliographer were to tell me that something could not be so because the publisher had neither record nor recollection of it, I would point to the time that Leonard Woolf denied the existence of a certain category of subscriber to the Hogarth Press. He did this when I had literally in my hand a copy of the first edition of Virginia Woolf's *Jacob's Room* in which was pasted a printed slip saying that this copy was for Mr. so-and-so "because he was a class A subscriber to the Hogarth Press."

If someone attempted to convince me that an issue in a binding lettered in gilt necessarily preceded an issue lettered in black—admittedly the normal and expected order of priority—I would answer by citing the case of Christopher Isherwood's *Lions and Shadows*, where the reverse is true, as I discovered when helping with a little piece of Isherwood bibliography.

In this year of all years, much play is being made with the colors of the two variant dust-wrappers on George Orwell's *1984*. One is green; one is red. Until Ian Angus and Ian Willison eventually publish the definitive Orwell bibliography, various assumptions are being made about relative priorities. My bookselling experience teaches me to be skeptical that there was any priority at all. I remember several occasions on which my firm's prepublication orders of a given title have been delivered in dust-wrappers of differing hues. It is worth mentioning that each time one of the jackets was green. The legend, for it is no more, that was passed down to me was that some booksellers thought green an unlucky color and were reluctant to use it in a window display.

Sometimes the curious practices of even the most respectable and eminent of publishers can muddy the bibliographical waters. In 1959 I was cutting my bibliographical teeth, as it were, by compiling a descriptive checklist of the first editions of Arthur Ransome,[2] author of *Swallows and Amazons* and recently the subject of an excellent biography by Hugh Brogan.[3] I went to see the man who was the dean of the British publishing community, Sir Stanley Unwin (then seventy-five and still regularly playing tennis).

He gave me access to Allen and Unwin's file copies, and I was immediately struck by the appearance of Ransome's 1927 publication *The Chinese Puzzle*. The book is by no means common and at that time the only other copy I had seen was at what was then the British Museum, which we are now having to learn to call the British Library. Sir Stanley's copy was in buff cloth, lettered in blue. The British Library copy was in yellow cloth, lettered in red.

As I gently pressed Sir Stanley for a solution to this riddle, he somewhat sheepishly confessed that it had been his firm's practice, at least during the 1920s, not to use a house designer to design a book's binding but instead to ask a binder's sales representative to submit sets of sheets put up in perhaps half-a-dozen different styles. The publisher would then choose the one he liked best.

I don't suppose any one of us here tonight would have a particular objection to that, but Sir Stanley went on to admit that the copies in the bindings *not* chosen for the production run were used as the deposit copies for the British Museum, the Bodleian Library, and the other British copyright libraries, thus, without, let me hasten to add, any malice aforethought, totally falsifying the bibliographical evidence for future scholars.

I do not know how widespread this practice was, but the moral for the aspiring bibliographer is clear: do not place too much weight on the evidence of a deposit copy without testing it.

The advice given to novice book collectors, at least in the more old-fashioned manuals and primers of book collecting, is: "Make a friend of your bookseller. He can smooth your path and help you avoid the early pitfalls. If he can be persuaded to take a personal interest in your collecting project, then you have won a powerful ally." I suspect that most collectors—and all booksellers—would attest to the excellence of that advice. It has been an important factor in the formation of some of the really outstanding collections and has also forged some valued and enduring friendships, one of which, incidentally, is largely responsible for my presence here tonight.

If the maxim holds true for collectors, then it does so doubly for bibliographers. Given even a modicum of appreciation and encouragement, the bookseller will ransack not only his records but also the furthest recesses of his memory for information about unusual copies and for hints of avenues that ought to be explored.

Because he has seen other bibliographers encounter difficulties and even fall into error, the dealer is in a position to advise on a safe course to be steered. Because he is in touch with other bibliographers and will be discussing questions of technique and approach with them, he ought to be well informed about the state of the art. He should be able to speak of work in progress and to report on practices and trends. He is in fact capable of being an informal bibliographical clearinghouse.

He—and his customers—see and use a wide range of the newly published bibliographies. Their reactions to innovation and change can be both revealing and rewarding.

Booksellers have been full and acknowledged partners in a number of bibliographies (Carter and Sparrow's *A. E. Housman*, for example, and, more recently, Hagstrom and Bixby's *Thom Gunn*), but they have been invaluable silent collaborators in many, many more.

Bibliographers' Qualifications

As I look at the extremely varied standards of modern author bibliographies and some of the idiosyncrasies in the selection of information and the manner of its presentation, I deplore the fact that formal bibliographical training is relatively hard to acquire. There *are* professional bibliographers, to be sure. There are also scholars, often in the field of

English literature, who have taken a formal course in bibliography. But many of the books we are considering tonight were compiled by amateurs. Let me give you some examples.

The standard bibliography of Somerset Maugham was undertaken by a man who was the public relations officer for Bertram Mills' Circus; that of Hilaire Belloc was compiled by a bank manager; and that of Chesterton by one of Her Majesty's inspectors of schools. The Thom Gunn bibliography I just mentioned was the joint project of a bookseller and a pathologist; and, of course, the most celebrated amateur bibliographer of all, Sir Geoffrey Keynes, was trained as a surgeon and not in the art or science by which we think of him tonight.

When William P. Barlow spoke about book collecting here last December, he deplored the fact that "so few collectors publish the knowledge they accumulate in their years of study." He went on to say that "collectors are not scholars, and they often feel their inadequacy in dealing with scholarly subjects."[4] Granted that I would prefer a little greater uniformity and precision in the use of bibliographical terms, I think our brand of collector/bibliographers has done rather well.

As far as I have been able to ascertain, most of these amateur bibliographers acquired their training on the "sit-by-Nellie" principle, that historic industrial learning system in which the newcomer to a semiskilled trade sits by the experienced worker and watches how she does it!

What the Bookseller Asks of the Bibliographer

That having been said, let us consider what bibliographies represent to the various sections of their audience and, more particularly, what those sections require of them. To the collector, bibliographies are the rule books by which the game of book collecting is played. To the scholar, bibliographies are guides to where knowledge is stored.

The bookseller, however, wants a bibliography to tell him two things above all else. They are, in order of importance: (1) What precisely is this book that I hold in my hand? and (2) What title—and what form of that title—should I be seeking?

All other questions are subsidiary. Certainly he might also want to know how scarce a book is. This may mean asking how many copies of it were printed, whether it came out in time of boom or slump, if the printer or publisher went bankrupt, or whether the book was born into a hostile world, as was the case, for instance, when wartime paper restrictions kept editions small in the 1940s or when half the stocks of London publishers were destroyed in flames during the Blitz—a factor in the rarity of the early novels of Elizabeth Bowen and Joyce Cary, for example. He might ask, also, how early a book is in the writer's career, or how, in terms of publishing history, it compares with other works by the same author. These are the questions to which the bookseller needs answers.

Now I am going to make a confession that will, I fear, shock those dedicated souls who spend literally years of their lives compiling descriptive bibliographies. It is a rare event for me to sit down and read a bibliography from cover to cover. Collectors of any given author may do so—once—but the truth has to be faced: most of us use bibliographies as works of reference. We turn to them, some of us a number of times a day, for the answers to specific questions.

This makes it all-important that the information we seek is readily available to us in a form in which we can speedily assimilate it. The first requirement is, therefore, that a book we use have a clear and comprehensive index.

A. W. Yeats's edition of James McG. Stewart's *Rudyard*

Kipling: A Bibliographical Catalogue has an index extending to thirty-five pages in double-column. Titles of separate publications are set in italic; the other entries in roman type. The numerals that follow are in italic type if they indicate a main entry but in roman type if not. Unauthorized editions have a special symbol in front of the numeral. The numerals indicate pages, not item numbers. I use Mr. Yeats's wonderfully detailed bibliography perhaps four times a year. (Incidentally, I also use, in descending order of frequency, the Kipling bibliographies of Livingston—with its supplement—and Martindell, as well as the catalog of the Grolier Club Kipling exhibition, but that is by the by.) I cannot remember Mr. Yeats's indexing system from one use to the next and have each time to turn in frustration to the key. Would that a simpler, uniform system could be agreed on for all bibliographies! I suspect that what we really need is a two-part index, one for titles and one for general entries.

Then we need a consistent and clear pattern of enumerating the items. From this platform Dan Laurence has described the growing dominance of the "Soho formula," as practiced in the series of Soho Bibliographies that Rupert Hart-Davis launched in 1951. It is a good formula. Most of you will be familiar with it. It gives an "A" prefix to books wholly by the author under review and a "B" and a "C" respectively to books and periodicals to which that author contributed. "D" is reserved for foreign translations—and so on. We all know where we are.

It was irritating, therefore, when my friend J. Alexander Rolph departed from it in his bibliography of Dylan Thomas and gave his "A" numbers to what he termed "literary biographies of poems" and designated Thomas's first book "B.1" not "A.1"—confusing us all.

The new edition of the bibliography of Lawrence Durrell by Alan G. Thomas and James A. Brigham offends in a similar way. It includes translations of Durrell's books in

Section A, puts contributions to periodicals in Section E instead of C, and so on. What is worse, it lists 618 items about Durrell without giving them item numbers at all. Heaping Pelion upon Ossa, it even arranges some sections chronologically but others alphabetically!

That most revered of contemporary bibliographers, Donald Gallup, for whose work on Eliot and Pound we all have cause to bless his name, had to face a dilemma concerning the consistency of numbering. Between the first and second editions of his Eliot bibliography he discovered fresh information about the priority of two books published in August 1942. He therefore reversed the order of their listing and gave each its correct number in the revised chronological sequence—the number that had previously belonged to the other. Thus "Gallup A40" now refers to *The Classics and the Man of Letters* and not *The Music of Poetry*. This might seem of very little consequence, but when collectors use numbers alone to communicate their needs to booksellers in a kind of shorthand, inconvenience and confusion arise. In an era when certain of the newer dealers evince a compulsion to follow every catalog entry with a numerical reference to the relevant bibliography (regardless of whether the bibliography has anything in particular to say about the work in question), you will see the problem. The trend takes on a particular absurdity when in any case only one edition of the listed title exists. One assumes that the dealers who follow this practice are seeking shortcuts on the road to being adjudged "scholar-booksellers."

But I digress. The aim should be to retain the original numbers when a bibliography is revised. Of the obvious ways of coping with the insertion of newly discovered items into a previously established numerical sequence I dismiss two: the French method of designating the new item after, for instance, "A.24" as "A.24 *bis*" falls down if, horror of horrors, there is ever a need to insert a further item in the same spot. "A.24 *ter*" or "A.24 *trois* fois" would sound absurd! I dislike adding letters in the fashion of "A.24a" or "A.24b" because letter-suffixes to bibliographical numbers tend to have a totally different significance anyway. I opt for the simple solution of using the slash or oblique stroke to give for example, a sequence of "A.24," "A.24/1," and, if necessary, "A.24/2" before "A.25."

Just as we expect the arrangement to be logical and the index to be clear, so we have a right to anticipate that bibliographical terms will be used precisely and in the sense to which we are accustomed.

It all used to be very simple. An edition was the number of copies run off from one setting of type. An impression was the number of copies run off at any one time. An issue was a postpublication variant within an impression. A state was a variant before publication. (I take my definitions as loose paraphrases from John Carter's *ABC for Book Collectors*, but Fredson Bowers's *Principles of Bibliographical Description* does not differ materially).

Now two members of what I call the Columbia school of bibliography (not a New York establishment presided over by Mr. Terry Belanger but a more loosely knit group of scholars on the campus of the University of South Carolina) are threatening to change all that. In an article in *Proof; the Yearbook of American Bibliographical and Textual Studies*, James B. Meriwether and Joseph Katz argued for "A Redefinition of 'Issue,'" attempting to restrict the use of the word to the publishing history of a book, while reserving "state" for the printing history.[5] This is not the place to rehearse their arguments, or to go further into the intricacies of that particular question. Suffice it to say that I have much sympathy with their case that *issue* and *state* used in the old way are less than satisfactory for describing some of the vagaries of production and publication in the age of the machine-made book, but here I come back to my point that we need to be able to open a reference book at a given entry and to extract the desired information quickly and easily. It is not sufficient to write an introduction, however well-reasoned, telling us that in this particular bibliography old words will be given a new meaning, for we read the introduction once, when the bibliography first comes into our hands, not each time we want to look up one title.

In short, I want bibliographers to find other ways of coping with the problems posed by machine-made books than by tampering with existing definitions. New terms may be needed. For example, in his bibliography of Flannery O'Connor, David Farmer uses the term *plating* to indicate "the offset plate prepared for each printing job rather than a stereotype or electrotype plate" such as would have been used "in late nineteenth or early twentieth century book production." Thus Farmer's "first plating" would cover all the impressions produced from one set of offset plates.

As well as abiding by precise definitions of bibliographical terms, my ideal bibliographer defines for us the precise standards to which he is working. In the Engelhard lecture already referred to, William P. Barlow said in a different context that multiple copies were essential "not only to provide a copy of each known state but to search for unknown states." Precisely, but unless the known is most meticulously described, we shall not be aware that we have happened on the unknown.

Let me give an example, A bibliography tells me that the page size of a certain book is 7 by 4½ inches. I measure a newly acquired copy and find it is only 6⅞ inches tall. Have I found an unrecorded variant? If the bibliographer has stated that he has worked to the nearest eighth of an inch, I have; if to the nearest quarter of an inch, I probably have not. If he has not declared his standard of measurement at all, we may never know.

What is the optimum standard? The nearest quarter? The nearest eighth? The nearest tenth? In bibliographical terms, one-tenth of an inch is getting dangerously small. One hazard is the difficulty of using rulers or tapes which, like most that are commonly sold, have an uncalibrated "buffer zone," as it were, at each end. (Have you tried measuring the page-width of a bound book with one of those?) Another is the relatively uncharted way in which paper responds to change in humidity: it is entirely possible for shrinkage to occur.

An alternative to working in inches, to which I suspect we shall increasingly turn, is to use metric measurements. Here unfamiliarity is our only enemy. When I mentioned a page that was 7 by 4½ inches, everyone could visualize it. I doubt if that would have been the case if I had spoken of one 18 by 11.3 centimeters. Even so, I would be prepared to go along with centimeters, but the day bibliographers speak of 180 by 113 millimeters I shall throw in the sponge.

The next piece of precision that I look for when testing a bibliography is in its treatment of color, more specifically the color of the binding. Happily we have moved forward from the day when one of the illustrious bibliographers I have mentioned tonight (I shall leave you to guess which one) stated in print that the second issue of such-and-such was easily recognized because it was bound in cloth of a paler blue! His comment was valid if one was faced with the two issues at one and the same time, but otherwise it was not very helpful. Paler than what? He did not enlighten us.

We need a color code to work from. B. J. Kirkpatrick in her *Bibliography of Virginia Woolf* apparently used a standard, but she did not say what it was. In reviewing her book, I suggested that it might well have been a shade card for embroidery silks. It named nine shades of green—bright green, bright moss green, bright jade green, jade green, and just plain green were some of them—the different nuances of which were quite beyond my masculine comprehension. Raymond Toole-Stott, Somerset Maugham's bibliographer, recognized the problem and attempted to solve it by applying the British Standard for paints. This standard also has a somewhat esoteric nomenclature—and in any case paint colors seem to represent a narrower range of possibilities of shades than do cloth dyes.

The best answer so far has come from Thomas Tanselle, who has argued for the use of the ISCC-NBS Centroid Color Chart issued by the Inter-Society Color Council of the National Bureau of Standards.[6] Not even this is free of snags. Whatever standard is adopted must be easily accessible to users of bibliographies—and the ISCC chart is relatively hard to get hold of, particularly in the United Kingdom. Its color chips are quite small and, as Tanselle has pointed out, they "are glossy and book cloth is not." A despairing English bibliographer once remarked to me that he had never found even one binding cloth which exactly matched the Centroid chip. (It is interesting to note that Matthew Bruccoli, who declared in the introduction to his Fitzgerald bibliography in 1972, "I am color-blind," and who told his assistant to "keep the color terms simple," became converted to the ISCC system for his Ross Macdonald bibliography in 1983.)

There is another aspect of the problem that is even more insidious and to which an answer will be yet harder to find. It is the problem of aging or, more precisely, fading. James Meriwether, whom I have quoted above, discussed this with me in the context of his forthcoming bibliography of the writings of Joyce Cary, which I hope to publish. In the case of a scarce book that is now fifty years old, it can be difficult to find a copy in pristine state to compare with the color standard chip. Some colors fade notoriously quickly and, looking around my office shelves, we soon found a book where only those strips of cloth turned over the boards showed any vestige of their earlier glories. Indeed, Meriwether mischievously maintained that it would be necessary to soak off the pastedown endpapers to be absolutely certain that one was gauging the true original hue. His attempt at reductio ad absurdum on one side, there remains the point that there are many books of which users of a bibliography are more likely to see faded copies than pristine ones.

Undaunted by all this, I still feel that we need a color standard and would subscribe to any charity that would give every would-be collector and certainly every would-be bibliographer the ISCC chart for Christmas.

Supplying color charts or guaranteeing consistency in color descriptions would of course be an expensive undertaking, which brings me to various thoughts about the question of cost. You will have observed the not inconsiderable, and still fast-rising price level of published bibliographies. In my field of English and American literature of the last hundred years, what was a trickle of new work in the 1950s has now turned into a veritable torrent. In addition to new works there are new editions. The conscientious dealer has to have them all. He cannot, with prudence, even save shelf space or recoup some of his new investment by selling off the earlier editions. He needs good and bad alike, for it is a sad fact that bibliographical errors, once in print, continue to be quoted in perpetuity. If a customer writes to us citing an early or inaccurate state of knowledge about a book, we need to check the reference to be able to refute it from later information. (I shall have more to say about the problem of updating bibliographical knowledge.)

These twin sources, new works and new editions of old ones, have caused my firm's own reference library to grow fivefold over the last thirty years. Prof. Gordon Ray, speaking to the Fellows of the Morgan Library, pointed out the economic consequences of growth in this area, and of the rise in price of out-of-print bibliographies, for the new entrant to the book trade. If he is to do his job well, he needs today not just an investment in stock but also a considerable outlay in what are essentially the tools of his trade.

Producing bibliographies is necessarily expensive. They are intended to have a long life, and paper and binding must be of suitable quality. The challenge of printing transcriptions of title pages and full bibliographical collations and other complex and specialized data demands the use of skilled compositors and of more sets of proofs than are thought economic in publishing today. There seems little room for savings here, for in bibliography one dare not cut corners.

Illustrious publishers have tried to, Heaven knows. In 1972 my colleagues and I were shown page proofs of certain sections of the *New Cambridge Bibliography of English Literature* and were invited to run our collective eye over some author-checklists in the volume on the twentieth century. In one instance, we found so many omitted titles that there was not enough white space on the double-column page for the necessary insertions to be made. In consequence, a high-priced reference book, which ought to have a long currency, was published without them. I asked why we were not consulted earlier, why we had not been shown galley proofs, and was told—by one of my country's most respected academic publishers—that on grounds of economy there had *been* no galley proofs. I rest my case.

Since illustrations add to the cost of a bibliography, it is important that each one is made to count. They should be there to make a point. A good example is the plate in Carter and Sparrow's *A. E. Housman: An Annotated Hand-list* that shows two forms of the spine label of the first edition of *A Shropshire Lad,* photographed against a tape measure. Another is a facsimile reproduction in Dan Laurence's *Bernard Shaw: A Bibliography* of some verses that are so far known only in manuscript and in proof. Laurence hopes his reproduction of the surviving proof page will help trace the elusive book.

A less happy example is the reproduction in the latest (the seventh, in point of fact) publication of a Lawrence Durrell bibliography (the volume I referred to earlier when I criticized its organization).[7] Here a costly illustration is used to show the dust-wrappers of the four volumes that make up the *Alexandria Quartet*, which are not in themselves rare and which appear to pose no bibliographical problems.

Worst of all, in my eyes, is the decking-out of a quasi-reference book with colored reproductions of dust-wrappers, which seem intended to elevate it, if that is the right verb, into a "coffee-table book." I feel this has been done in the case of a more general guide than we have yet considered, Joseph Connolly's *Collecting Modern First Editions.*

That work possesses another feature that has left me profoundly unhappy—a price guide. True, it is not too specific. Instead it grades books into eighteen alphabetical classes. To each class it allots a price band. Class A is for books worth £3 and under and Class R for books over £200. Now Richard Purdy's admirable bibliography of Thomas Hardy tells us, inter alia, that whereas the first printing of *Satires of Circumstance*, 1914, consisted of two thousand copies, five thousand were printed of *Winter Words*, eight years later. In the absence of knowledge of any peculiar mishaps (warehouse fires, suppression because of libel, and that sort of thing), it is fair to argue that *Satires of Circumstance* is two-and-a-half times as scarce as *Winter Words*. But Connolly gives us no such information as this, and there is no evidence that his classification is other than subjective.

I suppose that the same charge could have been leveled

at Michael Sadleir when he gave tables of comparative scarcities for the works of some of the novelists he dealt with in his celebrated *19th Century Fiction*, but Sadleir was the acknowledged specialist in his field and at least he did not take his comparisons beyond the confines of one author's books at a time.

Even if price guides were to be reliable when published, and even if they took sufficient account of variations in condition (which have never been more influential than they are today), their currency is such an ephemeral thing as to make their compilation not worthwhile, the game not worth the candle.

But let us return to illustration. I believe it was claimed for Matthew J. Bruccoli's *Scott Fitzgerald* (University of Pittsburgh Press, 1972) that it was the first author-bibliography to give not a transcription but a facsimile of the title page and copyright page of each first edition. For Fitzgerald, it seemed to work very well. Instead of laboriously setting type to imitate the changes of face (roman, italic, bold, uppercase, or lowercase) and indicating line breaks and rules and devices, one simply made a line block from the original. Could this really be the answer to a bibliographer's prayer?

Well, maybe; but I would not put it more strongly than that. In the first place, there remains the problem of scale. If all the reproductions are the size of the original, well and good, but if the writer under scrutiny had a varied output (if, unlike Fitzgerald, most of his books were not published in uniform format by Scribner's), I foresee problems. H. G. Wells, for one, published books in just about every format you can think of, from foolscap octavo to quarto and beyond. It would be difficult, not to say extravagant, to reproduce those same-size. To reduce some, and, moreover, to reduce some more than others, rather negates the point of the facsimiles. In other words, a reduced facsimile removes the easy comparison between what the bibliography records and the copy you wish to test against it. (Admittedly Bruccoli gives page size below each facsimile.)

Again, it worked for Fitzgerald because of his relatively small output: 34 titles dealt with in the A section. It would have been a far cry indeed from that to the 142 facsimiles that would have been needed to follow Bruccoli's practice in the Winston Churchill bibliography, to say nothing of the 177 needed for Edmund Blunden and the 311 for Bernard Shaw. No, this is a useful advance but I believe it has a limited application.

The bibliographer's task is an unrewarding one. For the first law of bibliography is that the day after you publish someone will point out to you an imperfection in your work—a variant, an edition, or even, Heaven forfend, a title that you failed to record.

This law applies no matter how long your work is in preparation; no matter how assiduously you have sought out all possible variants; no matter how many libraries you have visited or collectors you have consulted. Always, immediately you publish, someone you had failed to reach, someone whose very existence you had not even suspected, will bob up with a new piece of information.

This is not perversity on the part of whoever so belatedly comes forward. It is the natural consequence of publication, for only when the standard, the norm, is defined can others be aware that they have a variant or an unrecorded item. Thus it is a rash bibliographer indeed who would be prepared to give odds against publication of his magnum opus being swiftly followed by one of those knowing footnotes in a bookseller's catalog that begins with some such phrase as, "not in Bloggins."

Given the inevitability of the discovery of new material, how is the bibliographer to communicate it to his audience? After a decent lapse of time and when sufficient addenda and corrigenda have been accumulated, it is reasonable to publish a new edition, but speaking as a book *buyer* and not simply as a book *seller*, and given the necessarily high price of bibliographies today, I would hope that "a reasonable lapse of time" might be interpreted as not less than ten years. I make no complaint, but I would respectfully point to the presence in my company's reference library of no fewer than three editions of Alan Wade's bibliography of Yeats, of B. J. Kirkpatrick's bibliography of Virginia Woolf, and of Geoffrey Keynes's bibliography of Rupert Brooke.

How is one to cope with the problem until a new edition is justified? By publishing an article in one of the bibliographical journals? Yes; but which one? *The Book Collector*? *The Library*? *P.B.S.A.*? I suppose it is true that learned libraries and most serious bookdealers subscribe to all these, but I very much doubt that the average collector of the work of, for example, Yeats, Woolf, or Brooke subscribes to more than one at the very most. And there remains the matter of seeing that the journals are indexed speedily enough to be of use and of cross-referencing the bibliography itself to the various pieces of information that update it.

A more romantic solution is to invite buyers of the original edition of the bibliography to register their names and addresses with the publisher so that a supplement can be sent, ideally as part of the contract implied when the purchaser pays his money and takes his book home, but alternatively on a cash basis. I said that this was a romantic solution for I can imagine few publishers cheerfully agreeing either to maintain a list of the names and addresses of subscribers to the first edition or to undertake the scarcely profit-making task of mailing out what might be a four-page or eight-page supplement every year or two. Here again the bookseller comes into the picture, for his notorious jealousy in the matter of customers' names and addresses might make the initial list of subscribers hard to compile.

And yet I suspect that there is an answer to the peculiar difficulty of updating bibliographies. We now have a machine ready-made, almost purpose-built, for the storage and retrieval of the latest information. As a man who thinks that the quill pen took us admirably far along the road to a technological Utopia, I hate to admit it, but that machine is the computer. Now "The Computer's Role in Bibliography" might make an interesting theme for someone else's Engelhard lecture.

Notes

1. Dan H. Laurence, *A Portrait of the Author as a Bibliography* (Washington: Library of Congress, 1983).
2. See the *Book Collector* 8, no. 3 (Autumn 1959).
3. Hugh Brogan, *The Life of Arthur Ransome* (London: Jonathan Cape, 1984).
4. William P. Barlow, *Book Collecting: Personal Rewards and Public Benefits* (Washington: Library of Congress, 1984).
5. *Proof* 2 (Columbia: University of South Carolina Press, 1972).
6. "A System of Color Identification for Bibliographical Description," in *Studies in Bibliography* 20 (Charlottesville, Va., 1967).
7. Alan G. Thomas and James A. Brigham, *Lawrence Durrell, an Illustrated Checklist* (Carbondale: Southern Illionis University Press, 1983).